Fr. Dave Pivonka, TOR

Joyful Sons and Daughters

Embracing the Father's Love

Copyright © 2025 Fr. Dave Pivonka, TOR
All rights reserved.

Published by The Word Among Us Press
7115 Guilford Drive, Suite 100
Frederick, Maryland 21704
wau.org

29 28 27 26 25   1 2 3 4 5
ISBN: 978-1-59325-726-2
eISBN: 978-1-59325-727-9

Unless otherwise noted, Scripture texts in this work are taken from the *New American Bible, revised edition* © 2010, 1991, 1986, 1970 Confraternity of Christian Doctrine, Washington, D.C. and are used by permission of the copyright owner. All rights reserved. No part of the New American Bible may be reproduced in any form without permission in writing from the copyright owner.

Excerpts from the English translation of the *Catechism of the Catholic Church* for use in the United States of America, copyright © 1997, by the United States Catholic Conference—Libreria Editrice Vaticana. Used with permission.

Design by Rose Audette

No part of this publication may be reproduced, stored in a retrieval system, or transmitted in any form or by any means—electronic, mechanical, photocopy, recording, or any other—except for brief quotations in printed reviews, without the prior permission of the author and publisher.

Library of Congress Control Number: 2024925813

Contents

Preface 5

1. A Good Father 9
2. Earthly Fathers 19
3. Sons and Daughters 29
4. The Holy Family 41
5. I Am a Father 49
6. The Father Waits 57

Conclusion 69

Acknowledgments 71

Resources 72

Preface

Over 150: that's the number of references Jesus makes in the Gospels to God as Father. This is remarkable, given that in the Old Testament there are fewer than a couple dozen such references. It seems that Jesus isn't merely suggesting an image for how we might consider God, but giving us a new and profound way of encountering God.

Jesus invites us to encounter God as Father, and this is a uniquely Christian revelation. None of the other major world religions would speak of God as a Father who desires to be in relationship with us. We are invited, as we hear in Romans 8, to come to God not as a servant to a master, but as a child to their Father (see 8:14-17).

This reality has a profound impact on our understanding of God. Our God is not some distant fearsome deity. Rather, Jesus reveals his Father as One who is looking for us, who invites those who are burdened to come to him. He is a Father who is compassionate, slow to anger, loving, and merciful. God is ultimately, as Jesus taught us, "Our Father" (see Matthew 6:9).

Given how central the Fatherhood of God is to Jesus, I think it's something to which we must be attentive. Do you see God as Father? What does it mean to you that your heavenly Father sees you? He sees you in secret and knows your every want and desire (see Matthew 6:6, 8).

Our spiritual life radically changes when we encounter a heavenly Father who knows us and loves us—when we experience God not just

Our spiritual life radically changes when we encounter a heavenly Father who knows us and loves us—when we experience God not just as *a* Father but as *my* Father.

as *a* Father but as *my* Father. We no longer define ourselves in any kind of negative way; we define ourselves as sons and daughters, as children of a loving Father.

Over the last nine years, I have collaborated with some incredibly talented people from 4PM Media to produce videos that look at how God shows himself to us. *The Wild Goose*, the first series, discussed the Holy Spirit. We titled the second series *Metanoia*, and it delved into who Jesus is. Both series are beautifully filmed and consist of me and a few friends sharing reflections on the Holy Spirit and Jesus.

This book is about fatherhood. Much of the content comes from the third video series, which we titled *My father's Father*. This is a very personal story about my own father and his desire to lead me to my heavenly Father. My father passed away in December of 2021 and left a legacy of fatherhood that formed me and led me to his—to our—heavenly Father.

I also invited some of my friends to offer their reflections on their own experiences of fatherhood—both good and bad—to help bring us into a deeper relationship with our Father. My prayer is that you are able to discover a Father in heaven who wants your good, a Father who is for you. I hope that you will allow Jesus to show you his Father and that you will be overwhelmed by God's goodness. May the Holy Spirit pour into your heart the love of God, which will cause you to cry out, "Abba! Father!" (Romans 8:15).

Fr. Dave Pivonka, TOR

1

A Good Father

My relationship with my father was one of the greatest gifts of my life. It seems that, sadly, far too few people are able to say this. I can only account for my father's profound presence in my life by saying that it was all grace. It's not that my father was perfect or that I was perfect, but God blessed me with my father, and I like to think that I was a blessing to him, too.

I've thought much over the years about what made our relationship special, and there are just so many things. But I think the vital element, what held our relationship together, was Jesus. My dad continually led me to Jesus, and Jesus led me to my heavenly Father. My dad knew that, in the end, what I needed most was the Father in heaven.

I'm well aware that not every father-son or father-daughter relationship is like what I experienced. But no matter what your story is, the grace that was present in my relationship with my father can work in your life and draw you closer to your heavenly Father.

This book, of course, is about God our Father in heaven. But running in the background of the story of God as Father will always be our own story of fatherhood, either as a father or as the son or daughter of a father. No one makes it into this world without a father; it's one of our common realities.

The intimacy and vulnerability and closeness with which Jesus spoke of God as his Father were profoundly different from anything people had heard before.

And so over the course of these six chapters, we're going to discuss both God as Father and our experience of fatherhood, in order to move toward a deeper understanding of the Father's love for us and the healing that can come as we embrace that love. I'll talk more about my own father, too, because his example has informed me both as a son and as a man, and it has deeply impacted my priestly fatherhood.

Jesus and His Father

Thinking about, talking about, or praying about one's relationship with God the Father is a difficult experience for many. While I did have a wonderful relationship with my father, it was not perfect. This often invited me to reflect on Jesus' relationship with the Father.

As we know, Jesus and the Father are both God, but in the Gospels, Jesus doesn't just come out and say, "Hello. Here I am. I'm the same substance as God the Father. I'm the same substance as the Holy Spirit." Mostly he speaks of himself in somewhat muted terms. However, he often speaks of God as his Father and of himself in relation to his Father. In the Gospel of John, for example, he says, "Righteous Father, the world does not know you, but I know you" (John 17:25).

As I've been praying about and reflecting on the Father, I've come back to this passage over and over again. "*I know you.*" Jesus knows the Father, loves the Father, trusts the Father. In all four Gospels, he speaks of the Father. What does it mean that Jesus had a Father? What does it mean that he was a Son?

We all learned when we were children that Jesus' Father is God. We understood that Jesus had a foster father in Joseph but that God was his Father. For us this is normal. But when Jesus spoke of this in his time, many of his listeners were scandalized. The intimacy and vulnerability and closeness with which Jesus spoke of God as his Father were profoundly different from anything these people had heard before—not to mention the way he prayed to him as Father and taught us to do the same in the Our Father (see Matthew 6:9).

No one is father as God is Father.

—*Catechism*, 239

The idea of God as Father already existed, primarily under the notion of God as Creator. But, as the *Catechism of the Catholic Church* says, "Jesus revealed that God is Father in an unheard-of sense: he is Father not only in being Creator; he is eternally Father in relation to his only Son, who is eternally Son only in relation to his Father" (240). There's something different in his revelation of God: "No one is father as God is Father" (239). When Jesus prayed "Our Father," it indicated something personal, intimate, tender. Jesus' desire is to bring us into the intimacy of his relationship with his Father.

I believe this is what Jesus is leading us to in Matthew 11:27 when he says, "No one knows the Son except the Father, and no one knows the Father except the Son and anyone to whom the Son chooses to reveal him." Jesus wants to reveal his Father to *you*. He desires *you* to have the same relationship with his Father as he does. This changes everything.

> When I think of the Father, I think of the magnificence and glory of God. But then, in a very human way, I think of the loving face of Jesus: the beauty of his tenderness, which is a reflection of the tenderness of the Father. He could be really strong and confrontive, but he could be so tender with sinners. With Zacchaeus, the woman caught in adultery, tax collectors, and people with leprosy, Jesus shows us the heart of the Father over and over again. As you see Jesus, you see his kindness and his gentleness. You get a sense of trust in the Father's kindness and gentleness.
>
> —Dr. Bob Schuchts

Our Father

Sometimes in prayer, we can begin to experience the revelation of the Father's presence and his deep love for us. In the Gospel of Matthew, Jesus says,

> But when you pray, go to your inner room, close the door, and pray to the Father in secret. And your Father who sees in secret will repay

The Father of all creation sees you. He knows every part of you, and he never looks away.

you.... When you fast, anoint your head and wash your face, so that you may not appear to others to be fasting, except to your Father who is hidden. And your Father who sees what is hidden will repay you. (Matthew 6:6, 17-18)

I love this image of the Father seeing me, noticing me, and recognizing me. I mean, isn't that every little boy and girl's desire? "Daddy, watch me!" Every little kid longs to be seen by their father.

A few years ago, I was leading a retreat for young people, and one of the teens was wearing a shirt that said "NOTICE ME" in massive letters. One thing I love about young people: at times they know exactly what they need and aren't afraid to ask for it. I think the deepest desire of every human heart is to be seen—and not just to be seen in a vague sense but to be seen intimately by our Father. To be seen "in secret," that place where we are afraid to let anyone else see. Yes, that's where I need the Father to see.

The reality that the Father sees me—he *always* sees me—is really important. It's a paradox, I suppose. We want to be seen, but at times it totally freaks us out. We must know and believe, in the very depths of our hearts, that being seen by God the Father is a good thing, a very good thing. He sees us, and he's not frustrated with us. He's not angry with us.

The Father of all creation sees you. He knows every part of you, and he never looks away. He knows when you're struggling, he knows when you're sad, he knows when you're hurt, and he knows when you're anxious.

Sinking In

The reality that God is our Father is radically important in our lives, and it's crucial that we figure out what that means and how we can reconcile it with our own experience of God.

Many people struggle with this fundamental Christian truth. Having been involved in ministry for decades, I can see the questions and the confusion in people's eyes when I speak about God as Father. They seem to sink into a kind of malaise as their minds begin to wander.

What God wants are happy sons and daughters—not slaves or soldiers.

—Fr. Jacques Philippe

A GOOD FATHER

Many people have shared with me that they *want* to believe in a heavenly Father who sees them, knows them, and loves them unconditionally. Who would not want to believe in that? But—and there is so often a *but*—that's just not their experience, and it seems too good to be true.

I'm reminded of Pope St. John Paul II's statement that the spiritual life is a journey, "a great pilgrimage to the heart of the Father" *(Tertio Millennio Adveniente,* 49). With all my heart, I believe this is true. We're all on a pilgrimage, and it's taking us somewhere. Of course we need to make sure we're on the right path, that we know where we're going. But ultimately Jesus wants us to know the Father—not some distant God, not some God who's out there somewhere, but our God who is Father. When we experience the love of the Father, it changes everything.

> I have always seen God as Father, but now more and more so, because Jesus is always leading us to the Father, and the Holy Spirit also helps us understand who the Father is. Jesus' mission and the Holy Spirit's mission is to help us enter into the mystery of the Father. The highest knowledge of God we can have is to know God as a Father.
>
> The Son and the Spirit are the two hands of the Father, through which he takes care of us. The Father is also the One who is the source of creation, the source of everything that is given to men and women. All the graces we can receive come from the heart of the Father. He's so eager to give us abundance of life and to make us free.
>
> What God wants are happy sons and daughters—not slaves or soldiers.
>
> —Fr. Jacques Philippe

For Reflection

1. Jesus consistently identifies God as Father. Why do you think he so often insists on this identity? What does this mean for you, on your spiritual journey?

2. Think about one positive experience with your earthly father or with a father figure in your life, and one negative. Take those moments to prayer and ask the Lord to give you courage and insight as you begin to ponder the impact of your father on your life.

2

Earthly Fathers

In terms of our relationship with the Lord, we enter the world as something of a blank slate. Other people and our relationships with them impress on us images of God—images that affect how we see and come to know God. When we look back on our lives, we can see many relationships that impacted our image of God, especially as kids. We may not even be aware of many of these.

Our parents, of course, play a critical role. The *Catechism* explains,

> The language of faith thus draws on the human experience of parents, who are in a way the first representatives of God for man. But this experience also tells us that human parents are fallible and can disfigure the face of fatherhood and motherhood. (239)

Here we want to look primarily at our relationship with our father and the impact that relationship has had on us. This relationship in particular can shape our relationship with God the Father.

The key to the healing of any father wound is to be found in Jesus' relationship with the Father and his invitation to enter into a relationship with God our Father. More times than I can remember, as I have been praying with someone who had an obvious wound in their life, they were not entirely sure what it was or where it had come from. They would say

I think that little by little, in the Church and in society, God will give us true fathers and heal what has been broken.

—Fr. Jacques Philippe

things like, "You know, this probably wasn't a big deal, but when I was six years old, my dad . . . " And then they would tell me the story.

Sometimes they shared something that anyone would be troubled by, while other times, it was something by which only a young child would be troubled. But here we are, forty years later, and that experience has deeply impacted the individual.

Sadly, for many people, their relationship with their father is very difficult. This relationship is so important, so central to our development as healthy, happy people, that a breach often leaves deep scars.

> The great tragedy of today is fatherlessness. Because so many in the world are empty of God, it's difficult to find the place where we can be happy—the home we need, where we can be free, we can be ourselves, we can be happy, where there is a father in a genuine way as God is Father. But I don't think we have to despair about this crisis. Christ has been given us; the Holy Spirit has been given us for renewal and for healing. And I think that little by little, in the Church and in society, God will give us true fathers and heal what has been broken.
>
> These are such essential values and realities in human life that God cannot abandon our society in this situation. God wants to save the world, and fatherhood has to be saved, too.
>
> —Fr. Jacques Philippe

Praying through Our Triggers

My dad really was an amazing father, but that's not to say that he was perfect. Dad dealt with some things by getting angry, and as a little kid this could scare me. In my adult years, I once heard someone yelling, and it "triggered" a memory from when I was little. It wasn't a major issue, but my response brought home to me the reality of the influence of fathers.

I've learned that experiences such as this are opportunities for the Holy Spirit to bring healing. When invited, the Spirit brings light and truth.

It's vitally important that the Holy Spirit be invited to bring grace and healing.

This is where I meet many people in prayer. Some men I have prayed with feel as if they are not enough, don't measure up, are never good enough. "Why do you feel that way?" I ask, and many of them tell me they had a father with a critical spirit. It didn't matter that their grades or their performance in athletics, band, or theater was exceptional; it was never quite enough.

Oftentimes men and women aren't aware of this struggle. It takes an event to "trigger" something in them that allows them to realize that something isn't right. Their prayer can then become, "Okay, God, heal this. Help me deal with this. Reveal to me who you are as Father, not just who I think you are."

This prayer invites people to be totally honest with our heavenly Father. "Father, I feel as if you're always judging me. I feel as if I never do well enough, as if you are always disappointed in me. I feel as if I'm never quite enough."

I prayed recently with a student who had a father who was very harsh, and she now struggles with her identity. I think she knows in her head that God is a loving Father, but she doesn't know it in her heart. She often feels like a failure, as if she never does anything right. As we were praying, I asked her to imagine the Father before her and God speaking to her.

The student was quiet for a minute or two. It was evident that God was doing something in her heart. "What did you hear?" I asked.

"God called me his beloved. But how do I know that isn't just me saying that?"

"Is it something you normally hear?" I replied.

She smiled and said, "No."

This student had a beautiful encounter with her heavenly Father, who sees her as his beloved.

It's vitally important that the Holy Spirit be invited to bring grace and healing. Whenever I pray with somebody, I pray for two things: for light so that we can see, and for truth. Because often our self-talk—the thoughts telling us "You're not enough"—are like the voice of our earthly father saying, "You're never going to measure up. You're not beautiful. You need to lose weight," and so on. The Spirit can come in and bring healing in those areas. God speaks truth, breaks the power of lies, and allows us to see ourselves as the Father sees us.

Many of us have certain areas of our life where we think, *This is just how it's going to be,* or, *This part is lost.* I believe that the Father doesn't want us to give up, but he wants us to go into those wounded places.

The Grace of Conversion

My dad and I were driving in town one day. I don't know where we were going or what we were doing, but I can close my eyes and see exactly where we were. We lived in Colorado at the time, and I had learned something about Pikes Peak in school that day. I told my dad what I had learned, and he asked me a follow-up question. I hesitated because I didn't know the answer. I had already shared everything I knew about Pikes Peak.

I'll never forget how my dad looked at me and said, "Dave, you don't have to impress me with how much you know or with what you do. I'm going to love you no matter what."

> I had a great dad—he was wonderful in so many ways. I have felt protective of that relationship, even when some of my ideas about God bumped up against my relationship with my dad.
>
> My dad worked hard—he was such a provider for the family. For us, though, it meant he wasn't around a lot while I was growing up. I think that's where that early message came in for me, that God is distant: "Your father isn't here. He's good, but he's busy and he's not going to be involved in the details of your life."
>
> —Heather Khym

It was such a moment of grace for me, and I have felt the impact of his comment throughout my life. At that moment, my dad saw me, and I felt seen. This helped establish my identity as a son who is loved by his father. Even when I got in trouble, I knew my dad loved me and cared for me. This has made all the difference in my life.

Everybody needs that kind of experience with the Father.

This wasn't my dad's experience growing up. He had his own journey. Dad was adopted, and his adoptive parents loved him deeply. But at times things were difficult.

> For many years I thought God was standing there with his arms folded, watching me from a distance—watching me suffer. He was listening but not acting. He could have helped me, but he didn't. And this misconception about the Father affected what I was willing to receive from him.
>
> I've been on a journey that has taken me back into those memories. At each memory, I've asked the Lord where he was and what he has to say about that time. I've sat there for a long time asking, "Father, what do you want me to know?"
>
> —Heather Khym

I am sure that the way my dad sometimes processed his anger was rooted in some of his childhood experiences. As he got older and entered into a deeper relationship with the Father, he changed. My dad allowed the Lord to enter his brokenness and bring healing, to the great benefit of my brothers and sister and me.

I am fully aware that the relationship I had with my dad is not everyone's experience. That's part of the reason why, when I've ministered to people over the years, I've been attentive to their relationship with their earthly father. I understand the importance and the impact of this relationship, and I want them to be healed where necessary. My one desire is to lead them to an encounter of the God who is Father.

I vividly remember a day in my childhood after I had played basketball and done the best I ever had. I scored thirty-something points.

My dad always came to my games, then he would tell me everything I did wrong all the way home. I hated it. But this one night, after I had scored all these points, I thought, "This is the night he's going to be proud of me." I was looking forward to getting in his truck and hearing him say, "Man, I'm proud of you. I love you."

I must have looked like a blithering idiot, because I was walking to the truck with a smile so big you couldn't have chiseled a bigger one on my face. I got in the truck and looked over at my dad. I was waiting patiently, with expectation.

Dad slowly put on his hat, cranked the engine, and then said, "You know, if you had gotten a haircut earlier in the week like I told you to, you wouldn't have been messing with your hair and you wouldn't have missed that free throw."

I was crushed. In that moment, I was thinking, "What? What did you say? No, this is when you're supposed to tell me how good I did and that you finally approve of me, that you love me."

I brought this moment to prayer recently with Dr. Bob Schuchts. He led me in a prayerful moment with this incident, and he asked me if I saw Our Lord in it, in my mind. After some time, I saw the door of the truck open. I looked over, and there was Jesus. He was so clear. He climbed in between me and my dad and turned completely toward me, with his back toward my father. Jesus looked at me, moving in my view so I couldn't see my dad, and he said, "Don't look at him. Look at me. He can't give you what you want, but I can."

This was such a hard moment because I wanted my father's approval so badly. But Jesus said, "You may never get it. He can't give you what he never had. But I can take you to my Father. And he can give you all of that."

—John Edwards

The *Catechism* says that the human heart is beyond our understanding, that only the Spirit of God can fully fathom the human heart (see 2563). It follows that the Holy Spirit can come into those places that are wounded and illuminate them. Through my own personal experience and also as a therapist and retreat leader, I know that people can have a transformation in their relationship with the Father that will have a significant impact on their life.

My connection with my dad and then disconnection from him when he left our family put a wound of abandonment in me. But I didn't see that myself. I had to walk into my own healing process to be able to see it.

The wounds need to be named and then healed in cooperation with the Holy Spirit and with people who can facilitate an encounter with the Father. The experience of an encounter with the Father is really key. This can happen in many ways: through Scripture, through the sacraments, through prayer, through community. But essentially, it's a real movement of the Holy Spirit.

The beautiful thing is that this experience begins to replicate itself. When we're loved the way the Father loves us, we begin to love like that. The cycle of hurt and lacking is broken, and something new is born.

—Dr. Bob Schuchts

For Reflection

1. It can be tempting to assume that our upbringing and its challenges no longer matter. But God the Father wants us to live in freedom. In what ways do you think the healing of your past hurts can impact you and your relationships with others?

2. Our relationship with the Lord is the starting point for our personal healing. Ask the Holy Spirit to open your heart more fully to God's presence, so that growing in grace, you might begin to see those areas where you need healing.

3

SONS AND DAUGHTERS

There is a striking passage in the Gospel of Matthew that captures a significant moment in the relationship between Jesus and his Father:

> Then Jesus came from Galilee to John in the Jordan to be baptized by him. John tried to prevent him, saying, "I need to be baptized by you, and yet you are coming to me?" Jesus said to him in reply, "Allow it now, for thus it is fitting for us to fulfill all righteousness." Then he allowed him. After Jesus was baptized, he came up from the water and behold, the heavens were opened for him, and he saw the Spirit of God descending like a dove and coming upon him. And a voice came from the heavens, saying, "This is my beloved Son, with whom I am well pleased." (3:13-17)

I like to reflect on the fact that Jesus was a son—and not only a son but a son who heard the Father say of him, "I am well pleased." It seems to me that there are at least two really important things here: Jesus knew he was loved, and he knew he was loved as a son by his Father.

I'm grateful that I have the experience of being loved by my father and mother. I loved being their son, being seen and recognized as a son of Bob and Margi.

Being the son of Bob Pivonka: that's part of my identity; that's what helped form me as the man I am.

Now don't get me wrong, being the Pivonkas' son wasn't all rainbows and butterflies. Dad was a doctor in a small town, and a lot of people knew him. I could rarely get away with anything! One time the police pulled me over for allegedly speeding, and the officer asked, "Aren't you Dr. Pivonka's son?" And I thought, "Oh, great. I'm in so much trouble."

There were other awkward aspects, too, like the fact that Dad always gave the sex ed talk in health class. Believe me, there are few things as awkward as sitting in sophomore health class with your own father going through the birds and the bees. It was the longest class ever. And of course, my friends would always let me know when Dad had been in their class for "The Talk."

I might add that it was difficult to fake being sick. If I didn't feel like going to school in the morning, Dad would come in and start asking me questions. I'd think, "Forget it; this is not worth it. I'm going to school."

But overall it was great being my mom and dad's son and my dad and I were always close. Maybe part of the reason for the special closeness was that we looked so much alike. If you saw pictures of us when we were young, you wouldn't be able to tell the difference. Now this is evidenced by our having the same hair (lack thereof) style.

Even our voices sounded the same. More than once I spoke to someone who thought they were talking to my dad. I'm not proud of that, but at the time it seemed like a good thing.

Dad and I had the same likes and dislikes and enjoyed the same hobbies. We loved Notre Dame football, baseball, fishing, and James Bond movies. When we saw *Field of Dreams* together, we both cried our eyes out. (It's a beautiful movie!) Being the son of Bob Pivonka: that's part of my identity; that's what helped form me as the man I am.

Forming a son or daughter is a very important responsibility for a father. The prophet Jeremiah uses the image of a potter to speak about God. I like the intimacy of the image—of clay being formed and molded. It's so personal and speaks to me of how attentive God was when he created me as my parents' son.

God has created us, and he delights in calling us his children.

> God made us for love. He made us to be loved and to love. This is what our hearts were made for. And they will be most fully alive when we experience that.
>
> I remember a time when we were at a restaurant when our kids were little, and someone came over and said to my daughter, "I know who you are." And my daughter said, "Do you? Do you know who I am?" And the other person said, "Well, I don't exactly know who you are, but I know who you belong to."
>
> There's something in that reply that speaks very deeply about our identity. When you know who you belong to, that changes everything. Through the Holy Spirit, we receive knowledge about who we belong to: we are sons and daughters of the Father.
>
> —Heather Khym

This word came to Jeremiah from the LORD: Arise and go down to the potter's house; there you will hear my word. I went down to the potter's house and there he was, working at the wheel. Whenever the clay vessel he was making turned out badly in his hand, he tried again, making another vessel of whatever sort he pleased. Then the word of the LORD came to me: Can I not do to you, house of Israel, as this potter has done? . . . Indeed, like clay in the hand of the potter, so are you in my hand, house of Israel. (18:1-6)

God created us male and female, Genesis 1:27 tells us, and like the potter with clay, God was very intentional about who we are, who he created us to be. Using another metaphor, Scripture says, "You knit me in my mother's womb" (Psalm 139:13). This is central to our identity as children of God; it's this that defines and establishes who we are. God has created us, and he delights in calling us his children.

Honoring Our Parents

If I had a dollar for every time someone mentioned how their father was not the greatest dad, I'd be a rich man. The interesting thing is, rarely has someone said, "I may not have been the best son (or daughter)." I believe this is worthy of our consideration. What kind of son or daughter were you—are you—to your parents?

> When I was a senior in high school, my dad left. He told us that he was looking for a new life and a new family, and he wanted us to be happy for him. He would insist: "I love you, and I want what's best for you. And so you should love me and want what's best for me." This created a real tension for me in trying to understand what a father's love is.
>
> My parents divorced, and I prayed novenas, one after another, asking the Lord to restore my family and to bring my dad to conversion. Nevertheless things got worse. One night in prayer, I made a definitive decision: "I'm not asking you about this anymore, Lord. I'm going to keep worshiping you and I'm going to keep praying, but I'm not going to ever again ask you to bring my dad back. I'm not going to pray for him anymore."
>
> One night, months later, I was saying my prayers in my room and an image of my dad came to mind. He was standing under a giant umbrella. God showed me that he was pouring out on my dad all the graces and mercy, everything I had asked and more, because God wanted his conversion more than I did. But my dad was standing under this umbrella, trying to make sure that none of that could touch him.
>
> At that moment I realized I had to keep asking. If my dad let that umbrella down for a fraction of a second, I wanted the grace to wash over him.
>
> —Katie Hartfiel

I appreciate having the story of the prodigal son to shine light on this. It's one of the most moving stories of an ungrateful son and a loving father. Beautifully, the love of the father is what ultimately changes the heart of his son.

What I think is worth noting is that we, as sons and daughters, have a responsibility to be good children. The *Catechism* tells us, "The divine fatherhood is the source of human fatherhood; this is the foundation of the honor owed to parents" (2214). The *Catechism* goes on to quote Scripture:

> With all your heart honor your father, and do not forget the birth pangs of your mother. Remember that through your parents you were born; what can you give back to them that equals their gift to you? (2215, quoting Sirach 7:27-28)

Being a father, being a parent, is tremendously difficult, and no one does it perfectly. You might find that your relationship with your mom or dad is extremely difficult, or perhaps you never even knew your biological mom and dad, or maybe your parents passed away. Regardless, it is worth remembering that we wouldn't exist if it weren't for our parents.

Forgiveness and Reconciliation

I want to be very clear here: relationships, any deep personal relationships, are difficult. No one is perfect. I consider my father a really amazing, wonderful dad, but that doesn't mean I was never hurt—and that there weren't things I needed to forgive him for. The truth is that forgiveness is a part of any ongoing, deep, personal relationship. This is true for us and for our parents as well. It's a key part of the healing process.

> Forgiveness isn't whitewashing. Forgiveness isn't excusing. It's naming the hurt and feeling the pain of it—and being angry, being sad, recognizing the cost. And then recognizing how we've turned that unforgiveness into judgments and bitterness. That needs to be acknowledged and brought into the light and released—let go of—as part of forgiveness.
>
> Then we can go to the cross, and we bring that person to the cross and hear Jesus speak those words, "Father, forgive them, they know not what they do" (Luke 23:24). And then we can receive the person as the one who needs to both forgive and be forgiven.
>
> —Dr. Bob Schuchts

One simple exercise I encourage is to take a blank piece of paper and write, "I forgive you, Dad (Mom, myself). I forgive you for ___." And then just write. Let the Holy Spirit lead you and open your heart to God's grace.

A few things are helpful to keep in mind about forgiveness. Forgiveness is not a feeling; it's a decision. We forgive because we have been forgiven. And true, authentic forgiveness takes time and patience—it's almost never "one and done." But that first time is often essential: it breaks down the wall, allowing God's love and healing to pour into our hearts.

One simple exercise I encourage is to take a blank piece of paper and write, "I forgive you, Dad (Mom, myself). I forgive you for ___." And then just write. Let the Holy Spirit lead you and open your heart to God's grace. This simple exercise can be a healing experience. Tremendous healing is often the grace of forgiveness.

> Soon after my dad died, I went to Confession. I knew that, though my dad had failed me in many ways, I failed him in ways, too. I carried guilt for the things I failed to do or say in order to love him better and to reach out to him.
>
> But the priest said, firmly and lovingly, "You are here today because you want your dad to be in heaven. This is what you desire for your dad. That's all I need to know about where your heart is. And now what you are tasked to do is what you're doing today: pray for him. And the prayers that you pray for him now, the ways that you sacrifice for him now, and the ways that you love him now are maybe even more powerful than what you could have done before.
>
> "Imagine the apostles on the day after Jesus died. You want to talk about guilt! They're all thinking of the ways that they failed the Lord. The apostles were in the upper room where, the Gospel of John says, they had locked the door in fear."
>
> The priest continued, "Imagine these walls in your heart that are like the walls of that upper room. When Jesus walked through the walls to the upper room that day, what did he say to the apostles? He said, 'Peace be with you' (John 20:19). And the Lord wants to walk through the walls of your heart today. He wants to say, 'Peace be with you.' Peace in the ways that your father hurt you, peace in the ways that you failed him. But now the real work begins as you love him into purgation, this final cleansing of his sins before God."
>
> —Katie Hartfiel

The human person is never going to know peace or freedom or joy—in their fullness—unless that person is alive in the Father.

It's important to point out that there's a difference between forgiveness and reconciliation. Forgiveness is what God commands each of us to do. I am to forgive as God has forgiven me. Reconciliation is different: it takes two people, and that's not always possible. So while forgiveness is always necessary, reconciliation may not be possible. We can pray for this, but trust that in the end God will bring his peace.

Finding Freedom

God desires us to be free. The human person is never going to know peace or freedom or joy—in their fullness—unless that person is alive in the Father, unless they're alive in the Son. "The glory of God is the human person fully alive," St. Irenaeus said. And the only place where we'll be fully alive, healed, restored, freed, transformed, and made new is in relationship with Christ, the Son of the Father.

This is where we're going to find our meaning and purpose: who we are and what we are created for. All of that is entwined in the reality that we are a son or daughter of the Father, redeemed by the power of Jesus. Without this, we are orphans without a home.

For the last two weeks of Dad's life, I visited him every day. During those days we talked about many things: some trivial, some so honest and real that it shook me. "I'm not afraid," he would say. "You know, I've been following Jesus for a long time. I've walked this road, and I'm not afraid."

I was alone with my dad when it was clear that his death was near. I was praying the psalms in the Office of the Dead when he looked at me and said, out of the blue: "And Jesus is going to present me to the Father, right?"

I said, "Yeah, Dad. That's exactly what's going to happen."

That's one of the last things my dad said to me: "Jesus is going to present me to the Father." In that sentence, my dad summed up the journey. My dad gave his life to the Son of God and was a faithful disciple of Jesus. Scripture says that Jesus will present us to the Father. In the end, my dad, who didn't know his biological father, was presented to his heavenly Father.

One of the other things my father said to me before he passed was, "I love you." Not a bad finish; not a bad finish at all.

For Reflection

1. If you have (or had) wonderful parents who tried their best to love you, have you thanked them for their care? If your parents were absent or in other ways created a challenging atmosphere, what do you think of the idea of honoring them, at least honoring them for giving you life?

2. What does it mean for you, on a practical level, that God the Father is attentive to you and created you to know his love and healing?

4

The Holy Family

Jesus came from a family. I know that's obvious, but the Father could have arranged this differently had he desired. But he didn't. Jesus had a mother and a father. I think it's wise to take a moment and briefly look at this family, at his mother, Mary, and his earthly father, Joseph.

Pray about this for a moment: God chose to come into the world for our salvation as the member of a human family.

Mary, Our Mother

We've talked a lot about fathers and the important role they play in our personal and faith development. I don't do this at the exclusion of mothers. They have a beautiful role as well, and Our Lady helps us realize that more fully.

St. Thérèse of Lisieux said that Mary is more of a mother than a queen. I like that, because I know how to approach a mom, but how do you approach a queen? What would I say? Would I bow? I'm pretty sure I would make it as awkward as humanly possible.

When I was a postulant in my Franciscan community, I attended a series of workshops and lectures about Mary. The speaker, a priest, stated

It occurred to me that this is what a Christian mother does: she loves her children and leads them to Jesus. This is what our Blessed Mother desires: to love me and to lead me to the One who can love me as can no other.

that Mary wants to be our mother. At the time, that idea rubbed me the wrong way.

I went to the friary chapel that night and wrestled with this. "Why does this bother me? I mean, she's the mother of Jesus. Why would that possibly bother me?" In the dark of that small chapel, I grappled with this idea that Mary wanted to be my mother.

After what seemed like an inordinate amount of time, the answer came to me. I didn't want another mother. It's nothing against the Blessed Mother. But I've got a pretty amazing mom, and I really don't need a second one.

My mom is an amazing woman: strong, resilient, loving, and most of all, faithful. Mom deeply loves Jesus, and she passed this love on to me. She discipled me and led me to Jesus, which is what the Blessed Mother would do. So in the quiet of my prayer time, I actually blurted out, "I don't want another mother."

The moment I said this out loud, grace flooded my heart. I heard, "It's not a competition, Dave." It wasn't as if Mary wanted to push my mom off to the side or to take her place. I received the sense that Mary wanted to actually make my relationship with my mom even better. The fear and anxiety that I was experiencing were not of the Lord.

Further, what came out of that time in the chapel was that Mary wanted to lead me to Jesus. It occurred to me that this is what a Christian mother does: she loves her children and leads them to Jesus. This is what our Blessed Mother desires: to love me and to lead me to the One who can love me as can no other.

As I continued to pray, the role that Mary would play in my life became more evident. She, like my dad and mom, wanted to disciple me. And why wouldn't I want that?

To reflect on Mary's strength and her longsuffering, her ability to hold on to the promises of God in spite of it all—that was a game changer for me.

—Heather Khym

> For a long time I felt like a bad Catholic because I didn't know how to relate to Mary, although I appreciated her tenderness as a mother caring for Jesus. I went on pilgrimage to Fatima, where I felt God's presence in a profound way. And I felt the Lord say, "I want to introduce you to my mother here."
>
> At that moment, I realized Mary was a woman of incredible strength. I didn't know how to relate to her before, because it seemed she was just meek and mild. But to reflect on her strength and her longsuffering, her ability to hold on to the promises of God in spite of it all—that was a game changer for me.
>
> —Heather Khym

St. Joseph, Model of Fatherhood

If our relationship with our earthly father is key to our relationship with God the Father, this says something pretty remarkable about Joseph. Jesus, who had a singularly unique relationship with God the Father and who is of the same substance as the Father, still needed an earthly father. He needed a father to be a model for him; a father he could see, touch, and hear; a father who could teach him how to build a chair or a table.

Young boys often do what they see their dads doing. I'm sure this was the case as well for Jesus. Jesus saw Joseph's care for Mary, and he saw his obedience to God. He witnessed Joseph's faithfulness and courage. What must it have been like to take Mary and Jesus to Egypt? Joseph did this because he did whatever he needed to keep his son and his wife safe.

I think we may be too quick to dismiss the profound influence that Joseph had on Jesus. Jesus was a little boy who needed a father. He saw and experienced what Joseph did, and it had an impact on him.

Ultimately the hole in their hearts can only be filled fully, perfectly, by the Father. But from a human perspective, it's also a role that a priest can take on as a father to the community.

—Bishop Joseph Espaillat

Here's the thing: If fatherhood wasn't important, then why did God the Father give Jesus an earthly father?

We hardly know anything about St. Joseph. We're never going to know most of what he did, although I think we can see the effects of his life in the life of Jesus. I think of my own dad who, like so many dads, did things that will never be recognized: the formation, the prayer, the intercession, the work, the toil. As a doctor, my dad would get up at 2 a.m. and go to the emergency room. He provided for us, we had a place that was safe, we had boundaries, we had all these things that at the time nobody recognized, nobody saw. But it's because of those things that I am who I am today.

As a priest, I've been able to relate to Joseph as the foster father of Jesus. For students who don't have a good relationship with their dad, I've sometimes served as a fatherly influence to help heal that hole in their heart. Ultimately that hole can only be filled fully, perfectly, by the Father. But from a human perspective, it's also a role that a priest can take on as a father to the community.

—Bishop Joseph Espaillat

St. Matthew presents Joseph to us as a man who was not interested in himself, who had a calling from God, and who gave himself completely for the care of the mother and child. That was all he was living for, and he wasn't getting anything out of it for himself. He wasn't getting wealthy. He wasn't getting pleasure out of this in any physical way. He was just pouring out his selfhood. And that makes him such an ideal model for all of us, whether we're spiritual fathers or biological fathers. We can take St. Joseph as our patron because he is the model of selfless fatherhood.

—Dr. John Bergsma

For Reflection

1. Do you pray to Mary? To Joseph? How might they lead you to a greater knowledge of who you are in the Father's eyes?

2. Pope John Paul II referred to the Rosary as "a prayer of great significance, destined to bring forth a harvest of holiness" (*Rosarium Virginis Mariae,* 1). Do you pray the Rosary? If not, how might you incorporate this prayer into your life?

5

I Am a Father

I can't remember a time when being a priest wasn't in the back of my mind. It's also accurate to say that I thought a great deal about getting married. The thought of being a priest was never motivated by not wanting to get married.

My mom and dad had a beautiful marriage and a dynamic faith life. I saw in them the beauty and goodness of marriage, and in some ways that made my decision more difficult. But it also reminded me of a key aspect of authentic discernment.

True discernment is always between two goods; it's not between a good and a bad. It's not something like: should I become a priest or should I work for a drug cartel? If I had married, I think I could have been a good husband and father. Marriage is a beautiful, holy calling.

I wrestled with this: what did God want me to do? I wanted to do what God wanted, but I was also influenced by my parents. I wanted them to be proud of me and to support whatever decision I made.

One time when I was in college, I wrote my dad a letter. I shared that I knew he and mom would be thrilled if I became a priest, and at times I felt this weight. My dad wrote back to me immediately, "That thought of you becoming a priest solely to make mom and me happy? This is not of

God. Tell it to go to hell." I was surprised at how direct Dad was. He went on to say, "The only thing your mother and I want is for you to do what God wants you to do." That is a father's love. This letter was profoundly liberating. It freed me to pursue God's will for my life.

The reality is that I think I'm a better priest because of my dad. My dad fathered me and he taught me to be a father. He taught me about love, discipline, patience, sacrifice, and mercy. I'm tremendously grateful for his example and that he was a constant source of support for me.

I must say, my Dad's death left a tremendous void in my life, but it didn't leave me feeling unmoored or adrift. I was asked one time if I felt orphaned, and my response was an emphatic *no*. This is because my father made sure I was anchored to the Father. He lived in relationship to the Father, and he wanted to make sure that I lived in relationship to the Father. And so, his fathering of me was never merely about him; it was always about making sure that I was connected to the Father.

Now I feel this same calling. I am a priest, a father to my community. As the president of Franciscan University, I experience a deep responsibility as a father, as a pastor over my community.

I often get nervous, wondering if the students are making good decisions. Are they safe? Are they staying on the path to heaven? I don't want them to do something that would compromise that, and I feel this weight to do the best I can to help lead them.

Sometimes that means saying things that I know are not going to be popular. I know parents have to tell their kids, "No, that's not a good choice. That's not good for you." In a similar way, the Lord has asked me to be a father to these people, to this community, and I have to speak the hard truths, too. Just as a biological father will have to stand before the heavenly Father and explain himself, I'm going to have to as well. Did I share all the truth, not only the things that are nice but also the things that are difficult and challenging?

> I didn't always think about being a priest. Actually, I wanted to be a scientist. But when I was eighteen years old, I went on a five-day retreat before going to university. During this retreat, I felt in a strong way that God was asking me to change my plans. He was fighting for me to give my life to him. So I had a few days of resisting. But after, I thought it was better to say yes to God than to say no!
>
> So when I came back to my home, I said, "I have to change my plans. I won't go to Paris (to this very good school I was supposed to go to); I will go to seminary."
>
> My parents were surprised. They were not expecting that at all. But they were okay. They were very respectful of my decisions.
>
> —Fr. Jacques Philippe

Priestly Father Wounds

I remember the first time I was confronted with the scandal of priestly abuse. I had been ordained for only two years when the media began bringing it into the light. Honestly, I was pretty naïve before this, and it just broke me. I remember sitting in a chapel one afternoon. I was crying and asking, "Lord, what do I do about this?" So many young people had been hurt; the sense of betrayal was horrific.

Over the years, I've sat with people as they've shared their story about being abused, and I've felt so inadequate, so helpless. I have often said, "I wish I could take your hurt away, but I can't. I'm so sorry." Many people have responded by saying what they want and need is to tell their story; to be heard, to be seen, for someone to be with them in their pain. They have thanked me for just being with them.

I wish it hadn't happened; I wish someone could have been with them in those dark moments. But what I can do now is be present to them, to listen and love them.

I'm reminded of a priest in Rome who was talking with seminarians. He shared that they inspired him because they're running into the fire. There are so many difficult things in the Church today. Like the firemen

There is a big necessity and thirst for fatherhood. So we don't have to reject this idea that one person can be an image of the fatherhood of God, and especially a priest with the grace of ordination.

—Fr. Jacques Philippe

and the police on September 11 who ran into those buildings, the priest is called to enter into the blazing battle. We can't run away; we can't hide.

> In France, as in some other countries, we have some people who say, "Today, because of abuses, we should no longer call priests 'Father.'" They think this way of speaking should be completely forbidden. But I think that's not good, because we have to find again a true way to be father. We need purification and conversion, but we don't have to reject this reality of fatherhood. It is so important.
>
> I can see in my life as a priest that many people have a need for genuine fatherhood: young people, teenagers, as well as women and businessmen. I've met so many people who have the need to meet somebody who loves them, encourages them, helps them to be who they are, and helps them to be free. There is a big necessity and thirst for fatherhood. So we don't have to reject this idea that one person can be an image of the fatherhood of God, and especially a priest with the grace of ordination.
>
> —Fr. Jacques Philippe

I think the evil one wants me to approach the scandal as if I've got to fix it all, which of course is a task greater than any individual priest could possibly do. What I know I must do is be a faithful priest who loves Christ, loves the Church, is faithful and is present to God's children in their suffering. I hope that this witness inspires God's people and brings healing.

There is so much suffering in this tragedy. I pray for the victims but I also pray for the healing of our priests, for those who have betrayed their flock and also for those who are faithful priests. They, too, have been wounded by this crisis. One of the biggest surprises for me about being a priest has been the level of sacrifice and suffering that's required, especially within the abuse scandal. No doubt God has been present and healing is happening, but there has been so much pain. Lord, have mercy and heal your people.

When my time is done, I pray that I was a good priest and a loving father to God's children.

None of this was in my mind or heart the morning of my ordination. I was awake early praying in the friary chapel. One of the friars came in and began to pray with me, and as we sat there together, I prayed what might sound like a silly prayer: "Lord, don't let me mess this up. I want to be a good and holy priest." In the end, this is my desire. I don't know why God chose me to be a priest, to be as a father to his children, but I'm profoundly grateful. And when my time is done, I pray that I was a good priest and a loving father to God's children.

> Thank God for good priests who are revealing the love of the Father to us. We need more of them, but we also need priests to experience radical healing in their lives. When a priest is passive and disengaged or making decisions out of fear, that's hurtful. I want to say to them: "This is not who you are, this is not who you were made to be, and this is not who the Father is." God the Father is not passive and disengaged. He engages, he pursues, he protects.
>
> —Heather Khym

For Reflection

1. Consider men who have been models for you of strength, virtue, humility, kindness—maybe your father, a counselor, a friend, a priest. What traits set them apart? Can you incorporate some of those traits into your own life? What choices can you make on a daily basis to achieve a similar level of maturity?

2. Why can speaking of your pain and suffering to another person be a step toward healing? Do you tend to bury your pain, or are you willing to bring it into the light in order to loosen its hold on you?

6

The Father Waits

In the beginning, God created Adam and Eve and placed them in the Garden of Eden, where they had dominion over the earth. They lived in freedom—vulnerable, naked, unashamed, unafraid. It's striking that one of the first things God said to them is that they were free: "You are free to eat from any of the trees of the garden" (Genesis 2:16). He added, however, that they must not eat of "the tree of knowledge of good and evil. From that tree you shall not eat; when you eat from it you shall die" (2:17).

The snake showed up soon after.

> Now the snake was the most cunning of all the wild animals that the Lord God had made. He asked the woman, "Did God really say, 'You shall not eat from any of the trees in the garden'?" (Genesis 3:1)

The first thing the evil one did was to cause confusion, stirring doubt in the minds of Adam and Eve. Did God really say that? The snake seized the moment. "You certainly will not die! God knows well that when you eat of it your eyes will be opened and you will be like gods, who know good and evil" (Genesis 3:4-5).

The contrast is striking. The evil one confuses, lies, and desires our death, while the Father who created us, who loves us, comes looking for us when we run away.

The snake lied. This was the first lie to infect creation, because eventually Adam and Eve would die.

Adam and Eve then clothed themselves. There's something significant about this: previously they were okay with being seen naked, but now they were no longer comfortable with that. And then, even worse, they hid from God.

What happened next is, I think, one of the most beautiful moments in Scripture: the Lord went looking for them. "Where are you?" he asked (Genesis 3:9). The contrast is striking. The evil one confuses, lies, and desires our death, while the Father who created us, who loves us, comes looking for us when we run away.

> The *Catechism*, speaking about original sin, says that our original parents fell and disobeyed God. All subsequent sin—the sin that you and I engage in—would be disobedience toward God as well and also "lack of trust in his goodness" (397). And that, to me, makes so much sense. Why?
>
> Because most often my sin is about me trying to meet my own needs. It's me trying to protect myself and achieve my own security because I'm not sure that God wants what's best for me. There's something about original sin that weasels its way into our hearts and allows us to distrust God's goodness. This is true even for those who have the best fathers in the world and the most secure attachments, because we all sin.
>
> Regardless, in God the Father we have a real image or template for a good, loving, trustworthy Father.
>
> —Dr. Matthew Brueninger

Wounded by Lies

Jesus says of the evil one, "He was a murderer from the beginning and does not stand in truth, because there is no truth in him. When he tells a lie, he speaks in character, because he is a liar and the father of lies" (John 8:44). Many of the struggles we have in the spiritual life are results of lies. When I pray with people, I always pray, "Lord, come with your truth, because your truth combats the lies. And come with your light, so that you can be seen."

Often we find ourselves in shadows, trying to hide from God. We don't really live in the darkness, nor do we live in the light. And we think we are safe there. This, of course, is a lie of the evil one, who twists the truth. He might say that because God loves you, he's going to accept you no matter what. This is true, but then comes the lie: therefore, it doesn't matter what you do.

This, of course, is ridiculous. Jesus says, "If you love me, you will keep my commandments" (John 14:15). We can't say we love Jesus and then ignore his commandments to love, to forgive, and to live for him.

To be clear, our behavior, good or bad, won't stop God from loving us. But it can stop us from being able to encounter his love. It blocks our ability to be open to the Holy Spirit, who helps purify our life and brings freedom over sin.

Here's another lie of the evil one: "You've already blown it, you're past help, the spiritual life is too difficult. You can't do it, you failed, you messed up, you're going to fall again. It's just too hard. Don't worry about it.

This is so like the evil one. Yes, it is true that the spiritual life is difficult. Jesus told us that it would be. He said that it's a narrow and difficult road that leads to life. Yet he tells us to pick up our cross and follow him (see Matthew 7:13-14; 16:24-25).

Jesus provides the grace to live this life. He is with us. The Holy Spirit leads us, God the Father shelters us. God is always with us on our journey, and he wants us to be happy. Even though we will have troubles in this world, Jesus tells us to "take courage, I have conquered the world" (John 16:33).

Of course we will fail, but God's mercy is always available to us. His grace and mercy always welcomes us back to the love of the Father. We don't define ourselves by our mistakes, brokenness, or sin. Rather we are children of God loved by the Father.

> I think we underestimate the power of the enemy's lies. The author John Eldridge says something like, "He's called the father of lies, not the father of ridiculous suggestions." And the enemy is good at it. God the Father is singing this beautiful song over our life, and the enemy is singing one that's just slightly out of tune but sort of intriguing. You find yourself trying to listen to it. It's enticing.
>
> I often find myself hanging on every word the enemy says. "Oh, tell me more about that, about who I am, that I'm not worthy, that I'm easy to walk away from, that I'm not lovable." I tend to hang on to those words, unable to hear the song that the Father is singing.
>
> And what is that song of the Father? According to what we see in Scripture, God is saying: "I have called you by name. You are mine. I'm making a covenant with you. I am for you. I'm coming after you. I will not leave you alone" (see Isaiah 43:1, Psalm 89, and more!).
>
> This is the song we need to hear, immersing ourselves in Scripture, asking God, "What do *you* have to say about who I am?"
>
> —Heather Khym

Father of Mercy

The story of the prodigal son in the Gospel of Luke is a story of a return home to one's father. In his book, *The Return of the Prodigal Son*, Fr. Henri Nouwen makes a powerful point when he speaks about conversion. I don't recall the direct quote, but the sentiment is that at times conversion is more difficult if you never leave home. In some mysterious way known only by God, this is what the prodigal needed: to leave home until he could recognize his need for his father. It's amazing how often this is true.

Nouwen also says that every one of us is the prodigal son when we go looking for unconditional love in those places and in those ways where it can't be found. And that's really what's going on with the prodigal son. He's trying to satisfy his need for love and his restlessness, and so he abandons his father and his home in a search that will only end in brokenness and despair. He has to come to that place where he knows his need for his father, for a home.

Our life may be a mess, in a really dark place, but whatever is going on, whatever the difficulty, we can always return home. We can run to the Father.

I suggest that there are many people today on a journey just like that. For reasons I don't fully understand, they've got to leave home. They've got to wander until they come to understand more fully their need for God.

The Gospel of Luke captures the prodigal son's moment of truth: "Coming to his senses he thought, '... I shall get up and go to my father'" (15:17-18). I love that image because it is the same for us: in our wandering, in our confusion, in our searching, in our walking away from the Lord, we come to our senses. And as soon as we come to our senses, what do we do? We return to the Father.

I imagine the prodigal son practicing his speech as he returns home. Part of him must be thinking, "My dad is going to be so mad." But he never gets to give the speech. "While he was still a long way off, his father caught sight of him, and was filled with compassion" (Luke 15:20). The father runs to embrace his son, then calls for a celebration: "This son of mine was dead, and has come to life again; he was lost, and has been found" (15:24).

Also, nowhere does Scripture say that the prodigal stopped off to take a shower on the way home after his time taking care of pigs. But still his father rushed out to embrace him—in the middle of his son's filthiness and sin.

Many people have found themselves at one time or another in a dark place—so broken, so lost. They experience this void, but then it's like a boomerang: they instinctively return to the Father. Something in the human heart constantly draws us to the Father. Our life may be a mess, in a really dark place, but whatever is going on, whatever the difficulty, we can always return home. We can run to the Father.

When I think about the prodigal son, I'm struck that the dad was standing there, looking out over the horizon, longing for the return of his son, watching for him every day.

—John Edwards

When I was released from jail after my arrest for drug possession, I thought my sister would be picking me up. But it was my father. I'm six foot eight and 270 pounds. My dad at the time was eighty years old, six feet tall, and out of shape, but in his presence, I felt like a four-year-old who's broken something in the house and is waiting to find out what the punishment's going to be.

My dad was looking at me, and I thought, "Well, let's get this over with." I walked over to him, expecting a slap or a shake. But he grabbed me and wrapped his arms around me, and he told me he loved me. It was the first time in my life I ever heard him say that.

He struggled. He asked me questions, like whether things that had happened were his fault. He said that he wasn't a good dad. I told him, "You know, Dad, you're a good dad. I'm a grown man. I made my own choices. You weren't always the dad I wanted, but what dad is? None of us are perfect, but you were a good father, and this isn't your fault."

And now when I think about the prodigal son, I'm struck that the dad was standing there, looking out over the horizon, longing for the return of his son, watching for him every day.

—John Edwards

The Older Son

The saddest character in the story of the prodigal son is the "good son," the older son. Part of an older son's responsibility during that period in history was to help restore his family when things were falling apart. If his brother wandered away or got into trouble, the older brother shared some responsibility for going after him to try to bring him back. Obviously, this older brother doesn't do his part. In fact, when he hears that his brother has come home, he's irate and frustrated.

The older son confronts his father about the party taking place to celebrate the prodigal's return. It's a profound moment. "Look, I've done everything for you. I've been here day in, day out. I've never left. I've never abandoned you or disgraced you. But not once did you give me a feast." He probably ticked off a long list: "You know, I tended the sheep.

I watched the crops. I kept the servants in line. And you've never even given me a goat" (see Luke 15:29).

This is often the case. The prodigal son leaves home, then comes to his senses and returns to the father. The other son never leaves home, does not know of his need for the father, and in the end does not participate in the celebration of the father's love. As Nouwen said, sometimes conversion is more difficult if you don't leave home.

While the good son was doing all the things he was supposed to do, his heart was not with the father. The father's response is critical. He says to his son, and we must let this penetrate our heart: "Everything I have is yours" (Luke 15:31).

I hear the Lord saying that to me: "Everything I have is yours." It's not because I always do the right thing (I don't), and it's not merely about following all the rules. There's nothing I can do to earn a seat at that table. It's the mercy of God. The heavenly Father's unconditional, perfect love allows me to have a seat at the feast. It's mine if I want to accept it.

The older son seems to think that he's supposed to earn his way to the table, that if he just keeps on doing all he's supposed to do, he'll earn his place. This attitude is the work of the father of lies, who says, "You need to do more, you need to do better." Many, many people are living with that lie: "The Father will love me if I perform better. The Father will love me if I behave better. The Father will love me if I do all these things."

The reality is that the Father loves you perfectly and unconditionally. There's nothing you could do that could make the Father love you more, and there's nothing you could do to make him love you less. The Father's unconditional mercy is true. It's true that he's pleased with you; it's true that he's your protector. You don't earn this, but you accept it and rest in it.

For Reflection

1. What does it mean that God "looks for" you, even when you sin? Are you willing to let him find you? Ask God for the courage to let go of your shame and accept his forgiveness.

2. Do you feel that you have to earn the love of God? If so, why? If not, what has given you the confidence to embrace his love even through the challenges of your spiritual journey?

3. How can you help others, especially those in your care, grow in the confidence that they are known and loved by the Father?

Conclusion

It's been over two years since my father passed, and not a day goes by that I don't think of him or feel his absence. A few months ago, I had an experience that brought these feelings back to the surface.

One Christmas my dad and I received matching Notre Dame football mugs. Well, I accidentally knocked mine to the floor. It shattered into countless little pieces. As I stared at the broken fragments, tears filled my eyes—not because of the mug but because of what it symbolized: the memories of Christmas mornings, football games, family breakfasts, and so many beautiful moments together.

That simple broken mug reminded me of the deep ache of losing my father and also of the overwhelming gratitude I have for the memories we shared. From fishing trips and playing catch to working in the yard and learning how to use a snowplow, my dad was always intentional about being present in my life. He encouraged me, disciplined me, and taught me important lessons.

One memory in particular stands out. After Mass one Sunday, I asked Dad about an image of the Holy Spirit above the altar. While people were filing out of church, my dad and I stood in a pew, and he explained that the Holy Spirit is always with me. I'll never forget that moment. God was using my father to open my heart to something greater than I had known.

As I've reflected on this over the past few years, one truth has stood out: I'm most grateful that my dad had encountered the Father in heaven and understood that this was the Father I needed most. A lesser man might have wanted his son to cling to him. It takes a humble, confident man to point his son away from himself and toward God the Father. For that I am forever grateful.

Since my dad's death, I've realized this even more. As the void he left in my heart has grown, it has been filled by the Father in heaven. He alone can truly fill that space.

Many of us carry a void in our hearts, and we live with that emptiness in different ways. It could be the way of the prodigal son, who left his father out of spite, only to return home after realizing his need (see Luke 15:11-32). Or it could be that of the rich young man, sensing a lack in his life and asking Jesus what he must do to inherit eternal life (see Matthew 19:16-22). Or perhaps we're like the woman at the well, whose string of broken relationships couldn't satisfy her deep longings (see Luke 15:11-32). Whatever that space looks like, the Father longs to fill it.

Let us pray with confidence to the Father, the Son, and the Holy Spirit, that we may truly come into our own as joyful sons and daughters of God.

Acknowledgments

As is always the case, there are countless people who make dreams possible. The video series, *My Father's Father*, would not have come to life without the incredible contributions of Dan Johnson, Jack and Jamie McAleer, and the team at 4PM Media. Their ability to take an idea and transform it into something beautiful is truly a remarkable gift. I am deeply grateful for the years of collaboration with Dan Johnson and 4PM Media—they are truly talented.

I also want to express my heartfelt thanks to those who graciously shared their stories: Dr. John Bergsma, Dr. Matthew Breuninger, John Edwards, Bishop Joseph Espaillat, Katie Hartfiel, Heather Khym, Fr. Jacques Philippe, Dr. Bob Schuchts, and Dave VanVickle. Your willingness to open your hearts and share your experiences has been a tremendous blessing. There is no doubt that our Father has used your stories to bring healing and wholeness to others.

Finally, thank you to the team at *The Word Among Us*, who believe that the world needs to know a loving Father.

Resources

My Father's Father

God is Father: this is the life-altering revelation of Jesus. Yet, how many of us struggle to know that we have a Father in heaven who knows, loves, and chooses us as His sons and daughters? Join Fr. Dave Pivonka as he journeys home to reflect on the urgent need to know God as Father amidst the backdrop of his hometown and the relationship he shared with his dad. This poignant documentary series explores the transformative impact of embracing our inheritance, unraveling the intricate tapestry of fear, doubt, shame, and brokenness to reveal a loving Father—for each of us.

Watch the six-part series at
wildgoose.tv/programs/my-fathers-father

Resources for Healing, Prayer, and Learning More

10thhourproductions.org/healing-resources

For other materials from Fr. Dave, please visit **FaithandReason.com**

10th Hour Productions

10th Hour Productions is a non-profit production company created by 4PM Media and The Ministry of the Wild Goose. Our films, series, and books invite men and women to an encounter or a renewed encounter with Christ who perfectly reveals the love of the Father by the grace of the Holy Spirit.

The Word Among Us publishes a monthly devotional magazine, books, Bible studies, and pamphlets that help Catholics grow in their faith.

To learn more about who we are and what we publish, visit www.wau.org. There you will find a variety of Catholic resources that will help you grow in your faith.

Your review makes a difference! If you enjoyed this book, please consider sharing your review on Amazon using the QR code below.

Embrace His Word
Listen to God . . .

www.wau.org